CZERNY-GERMER

50 Selected Studies
Arranged in Systematic Order by
HEINRICH GERMER

VOLUME 1, PART 1:
from Opus 139, 261, 599, and 821

Edited by Keith Snell

The painting found on the cover is titled *Pierrepont House, Nottingham, Nottinghamshire* (Yale Center for British Art, Paul Mellon Collection) and dates from around 1705. It is not signed and the artist is unknown.

ISBN-10: 0-8497-6370-3
ISBN-13: 978-0-8497-6370-0

GP445

CARL CZERNY (1791 – 1857)

Carl Czerny was an Austrian pianist, piano teacher, and composer, born to a musical family of Czech origin. He began playing the piano at the age of three. His father was his first piano teacher, and taught him mainly to play the music of Bach and Mozart. Later, Czerny took lessons from Clementi, Hummel, Salieri, and Beethoven. His first public professional performance was in 1800, playing the Concerto in C Minor by Mozart. However, Czerny never felt confident in his abilities as a performer, and decided to devote himself to piano teaching and only play private recitals.

In 1801, Czerny had the opportunity to play for Ludwig van Beethoven (1770-1827). Beethoven was very impressed, and accepted him as a student. Czerny remained a student of Beethoven for the next three years. He maintained a relationship with Beethoven throughout his life, becoming piano teacher to Beethoven's nephew Carl, and proofreading many of Beethoven's works before publication. Czerny gave the premiere performance of Beethoven's Piano Concerto No. 1 in 1806; and then in 1812, he premiered Beethoven's Piano Concerto No. 5. In 1846, Czerny published the essay "On the Proper Performance of all Beethoven's Works for Piano."

Czerny began his successful piano teaching career at the age of fifteen. His teaching method was fashioned after the pedagogical style of Clementi and Beethoven. He frequently taught as many as twelve lessons a day. Among his many students were several who became famous: Thalberg, Heller, Leschetizky, and Kullak. His most famous student was Franz Liszt (1811-1886). Considering that many of Czerny's students became piano teachers, he may be rightly considered the "father of modern piano technique" as his legacy was handed down through generations of students and teachers.

Czerny wrote literally thousands of piano pieces—possibly the largest musical output by a single composer in all of music history. He was the first composer to use the word "etude" as a title, and is known today mostly for his many books of etudes, as well as his eleven piano sonatas. However, Czerny composed many other works as well, including symphonies, chamber music, songs, choral music and concertos. Czerny himself divided his own music into four categories: studies and exercises; easy music for students; virtuoso pieces for concerts; serious music. (The music he termed "serious" remained unpublished, and included orchestral, choral, and chamber music.)

In a letter to Clara Schumann (1819-1896), Johannes Brahms (1833-1897) wrote, *"I certainly think Czerny's large pianoforte course is worthy of study, especially regarding what he says about Beethoven and the performance of his works. Czerny's fingering is also particularly worthy of attention. In fact, I think that people today ought to have more respect for this excellent man."*

Franz Liszt wrote, *"Of all living composers who have occupied themselves especially with pianoforte playing and composing, I know of none whose views and opinions are so correct. During the 1820's, he was playing exclusively the music of Beethoven, with an excellent understanding and an effective and efficient technique— to the progress of which he later contributed through his own teaching and composition."*

Heinrich Germer (1839 – 1913)

Heinrich Germer was a German pianist and piano teacher. He is known today for his excellent organization of three volumes of piano studies by Czerny.

The following is from the preface of the first edition of Germer's "Selected Piano Studies":

The development of modern virtuoso piano technique, as it has taken place since the time of Mozart and found its consummation in the "Viennese School," is closely connected with the work and influence of Carl Czerny.

There remains high and lasting worth in his piano works of an instructive nature—especially in his studies. Since they owe their existence to the lively, ever changing, give-and-take of practical piano teaching and show an awareness of pedagogical needs, they are marked by lasting significance, which remains undiminished even in the face of increased modern technical demands.

Czerny's basic principle in the studies was to set up in them the fundamental forms of piano technique by developing attractive themes in a not too complicated scheme of modulation, so that all pupils could thereby acquire technical facility and accuracy. This idea proved so practical for teaching, that Czerny's studies henceforth found their place as favorite material for piano instruction.

An up-to-date, new edition of Czerny's studies cannot consist of a simple reprint of the old first editions, undertaken in a spirit of misguided piety and destined simply to increase the volume of waster paper in the world. Instead, a strict selection of music must be made among the material that is available in such abundance, so that only what is genuinely helpful and at the same time musically valuable will gain admittance. This selected teaching material must then be placed in an order that represents a step-by-step, progressive course; and it must be formulated in a modern, instructive manner. The editor of the present new edition has followed these principles in the matter of selection, order, and presentation of the material. It is the editor's hope that the pianistic world will favor this new edition of Carl Czerny's studies, and that—to their many old friends—it will add new ones in its present rejuvenated form. He is confident that nothing but the most gratifying and happy results will follow from its use.

Heinrich Germer
Dresden, 1888

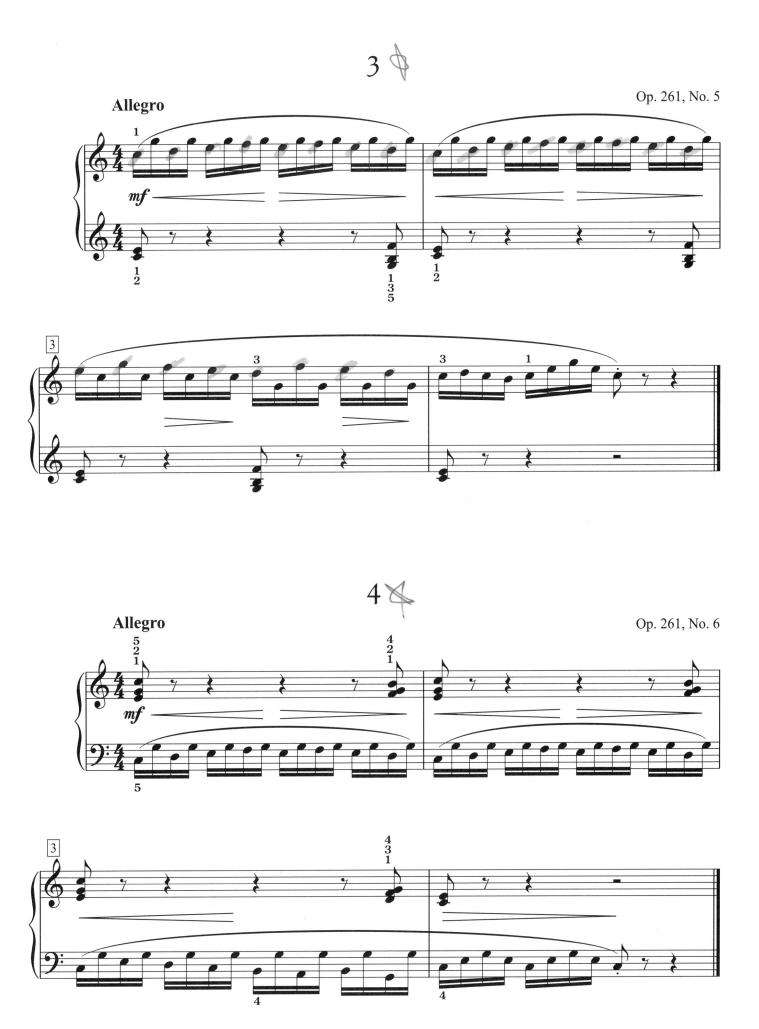

8

Op. 261, No. 23

9

Op. 261, No. 16

10

Op. 261, No. 33

Allegro vivace

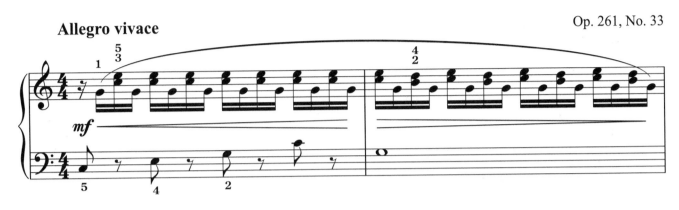

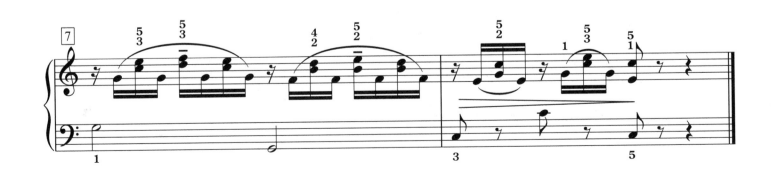

11

Allegro

Op. 261, No. 36

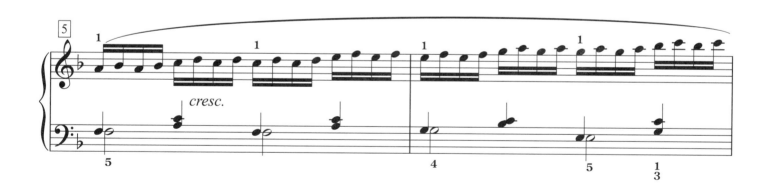

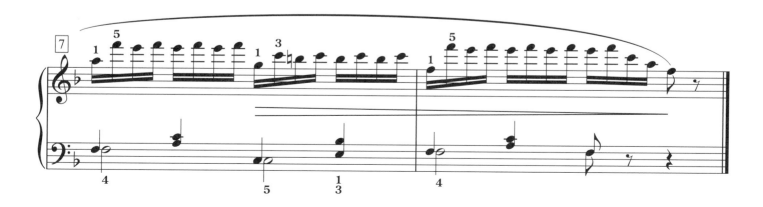

12

Op. 261, No. 35

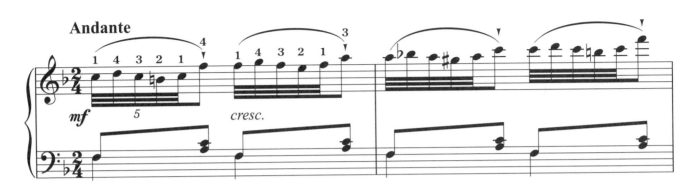

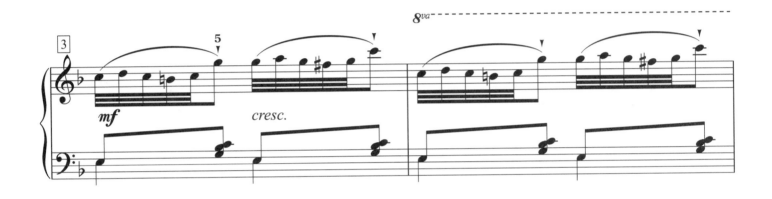

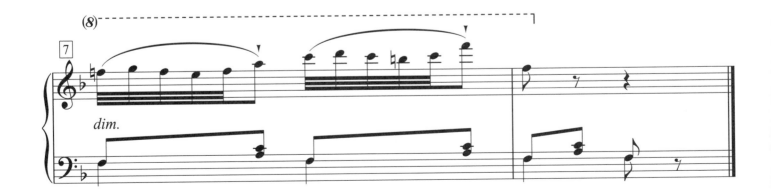

13

14

Op. 821, No. 1

15

Op. 599, No. 19

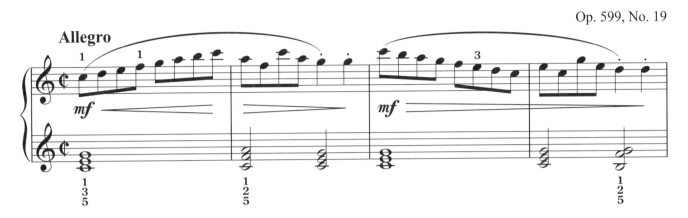

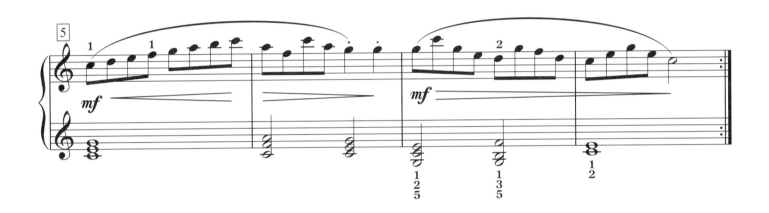

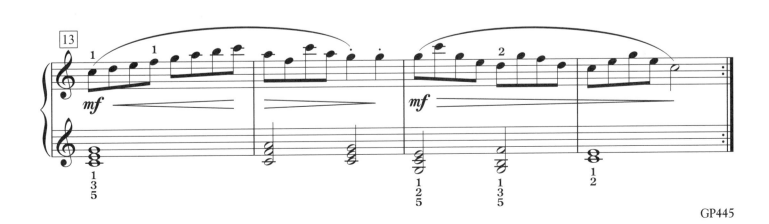

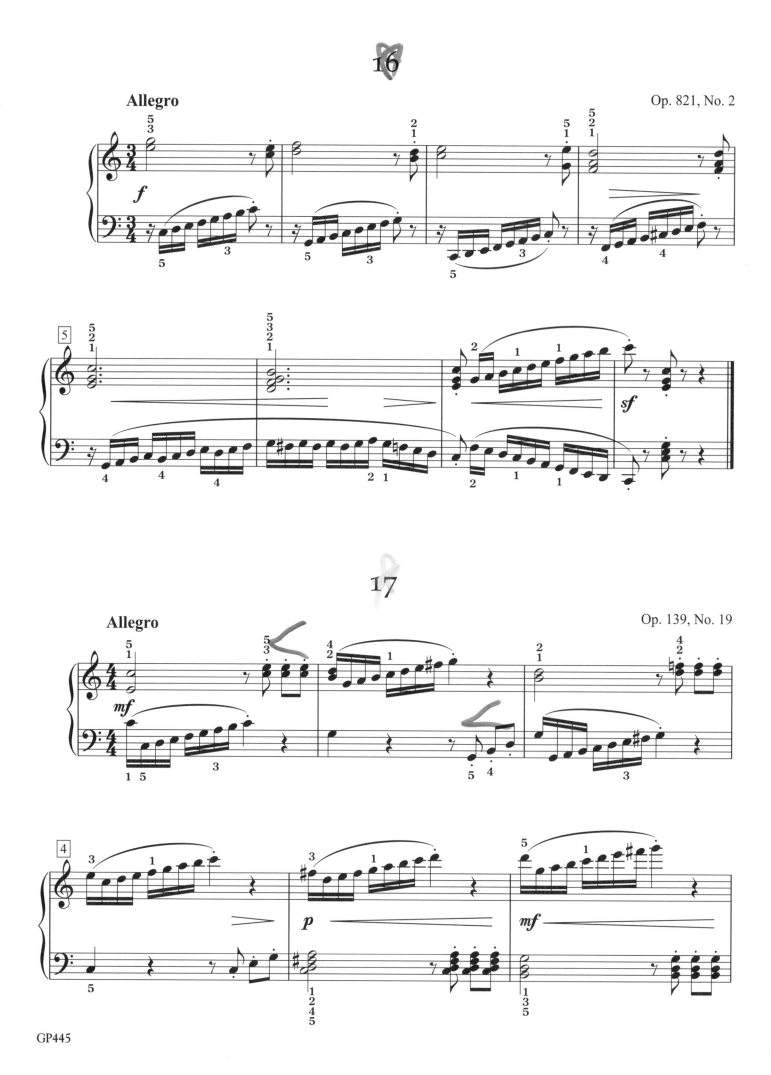

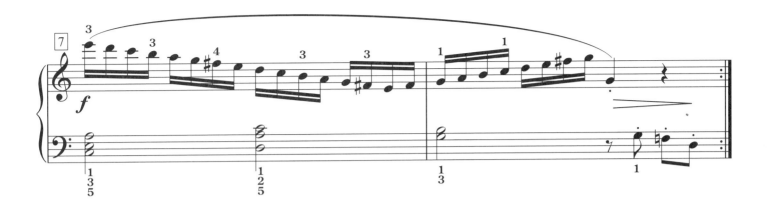

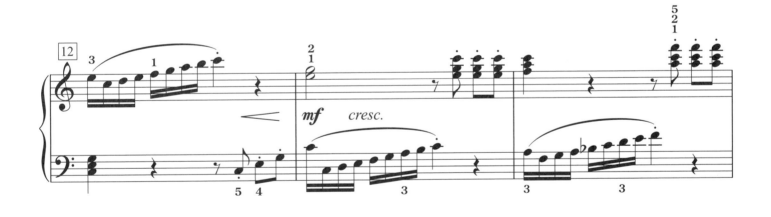

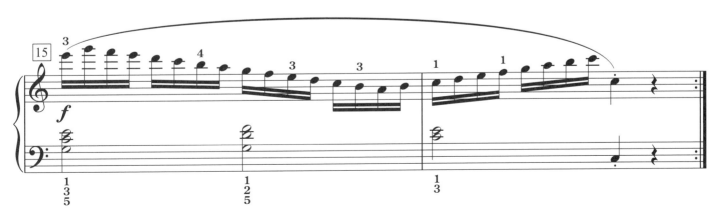

Op. 821, No. 10

Allegro

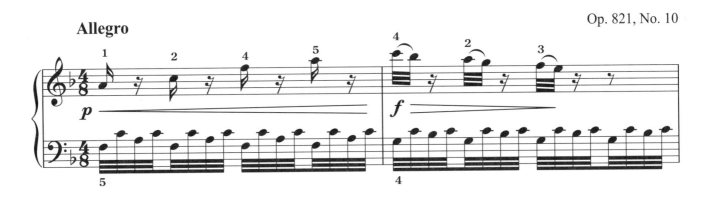

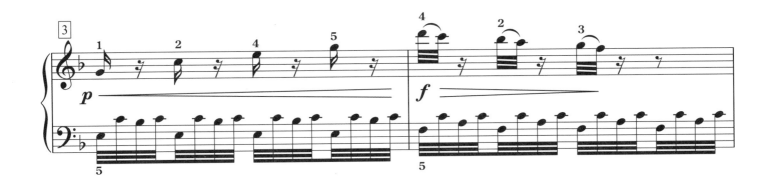

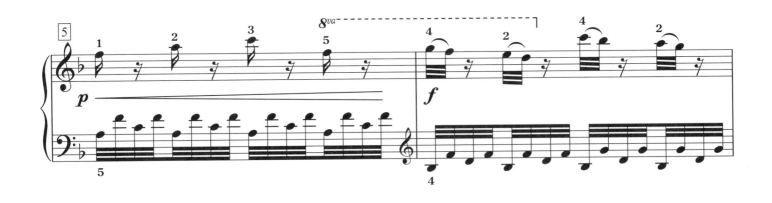

19

Op. 139, No. 69

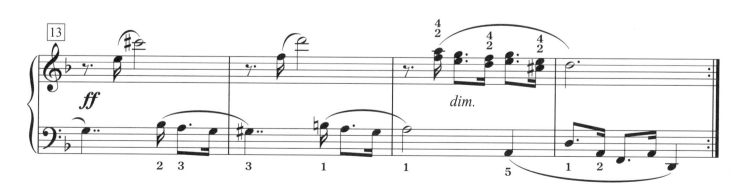

20

Allegro moderato

Op. 139, No. 15

(con pedale)

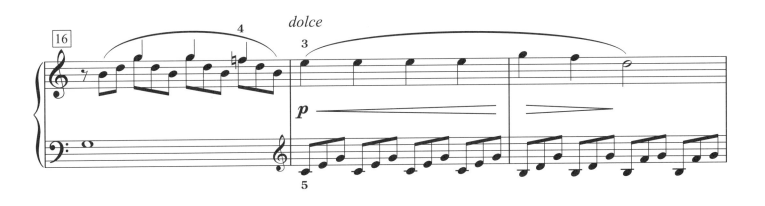

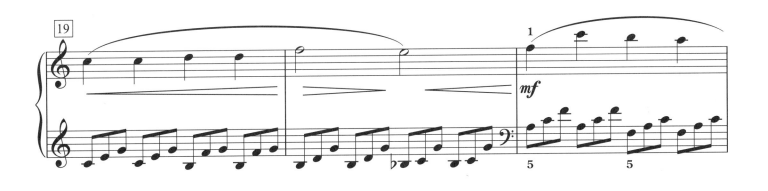

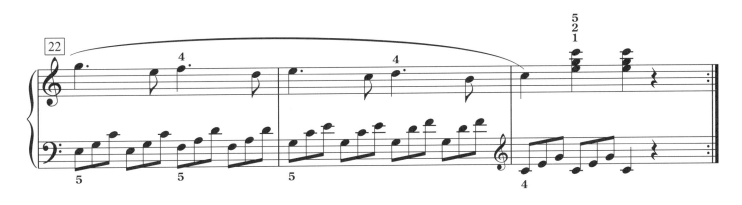

21

Op. 821, No. 15

Allegretto

22

Op. 139, No. 43

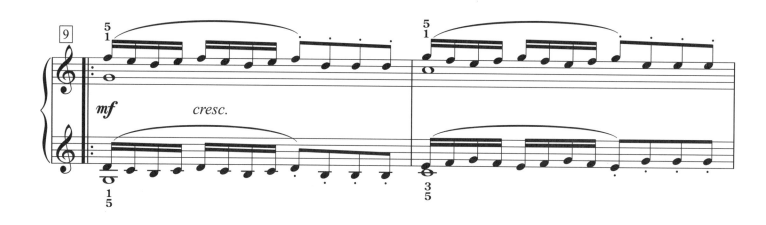

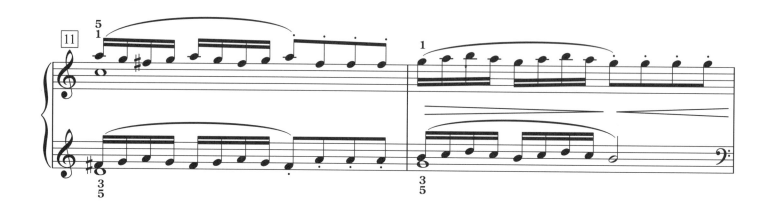

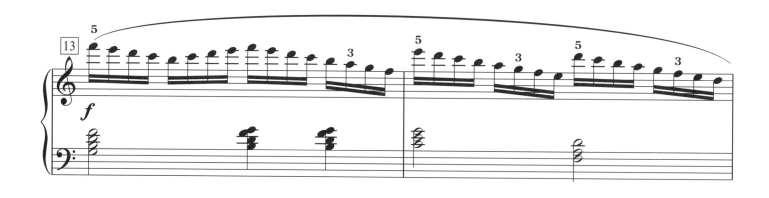

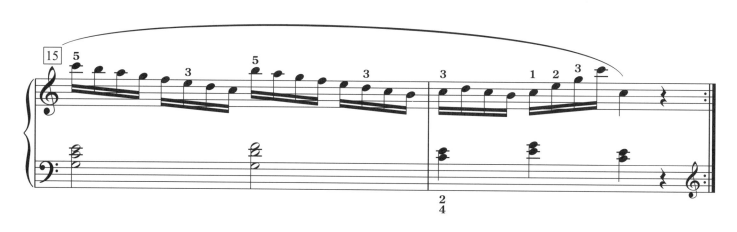

23

Allegretto

Op. 599, No. 45

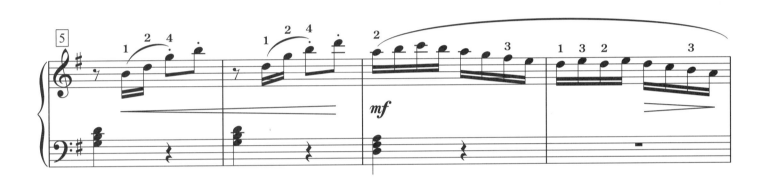

24

Allegro comodo

Op. 139, No. 42

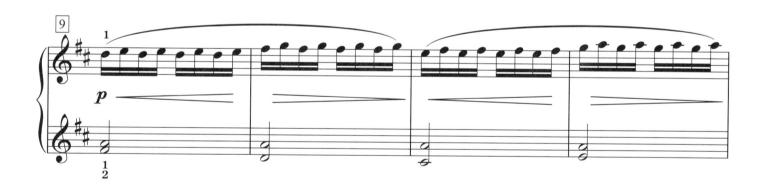

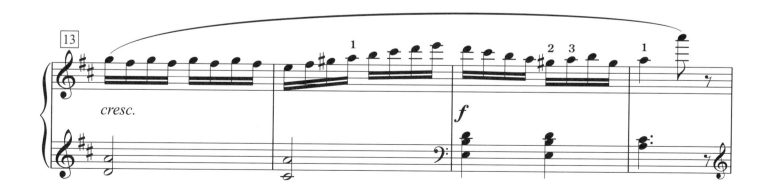

25

Op. 261, No. 20

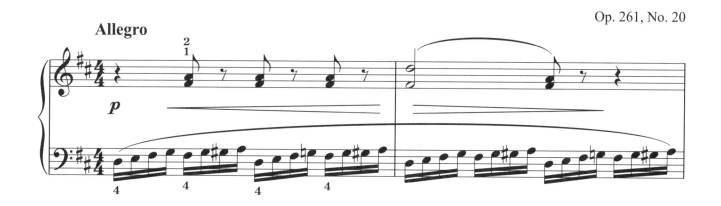

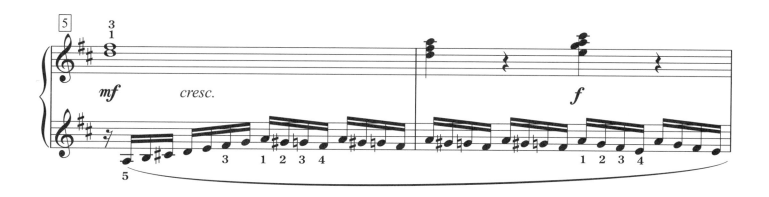

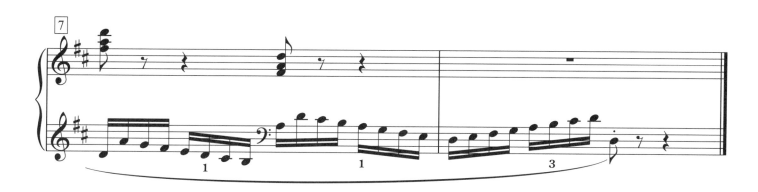

26

Op. 821, No. 22

Allegro vivace

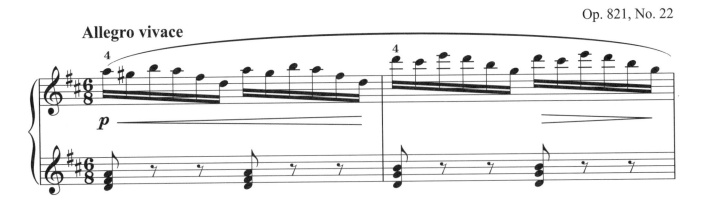

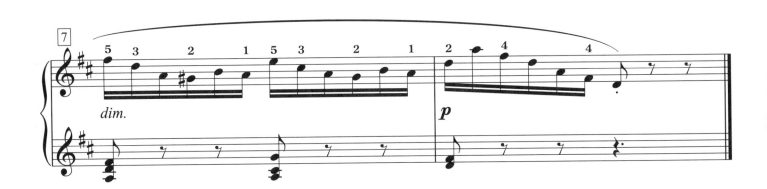

27

Allegro vivace

Op. 821, No. 17

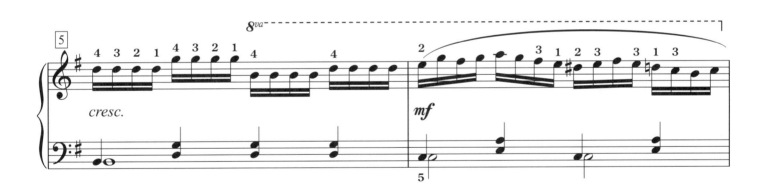

28

Op. 599, No. 63

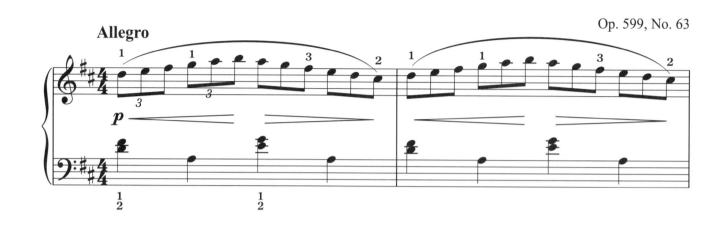

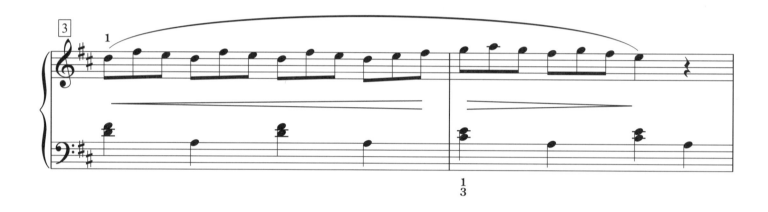

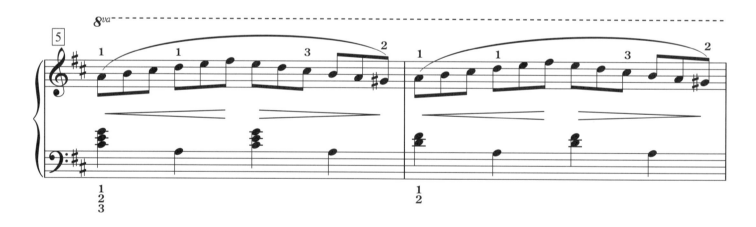

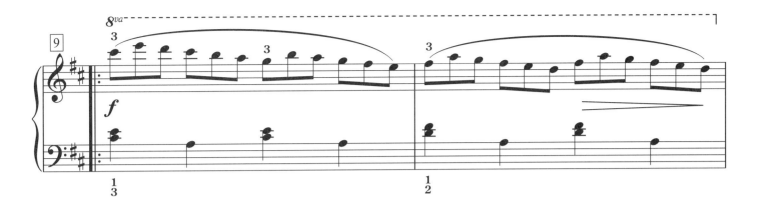

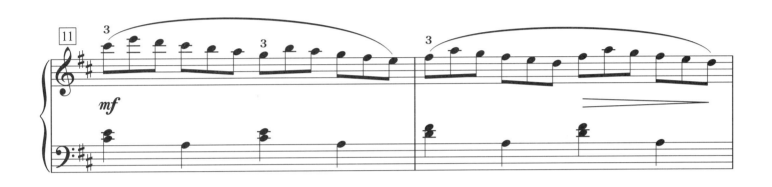

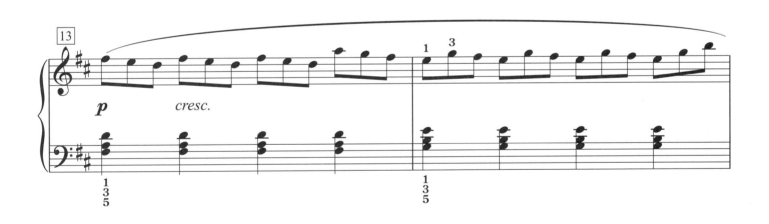

29

Allegro

Op. 599, No. 69

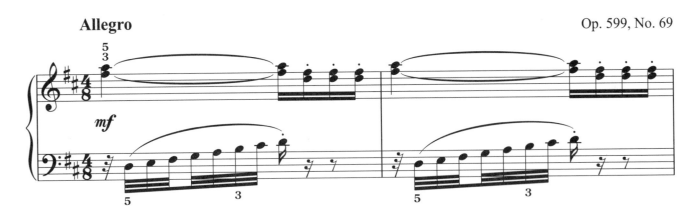

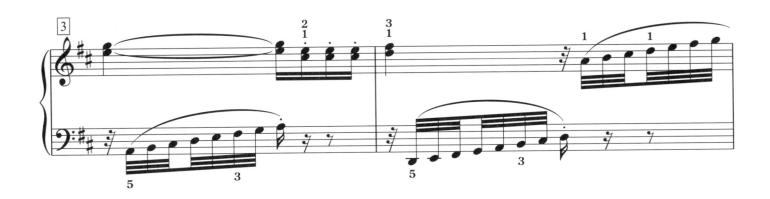

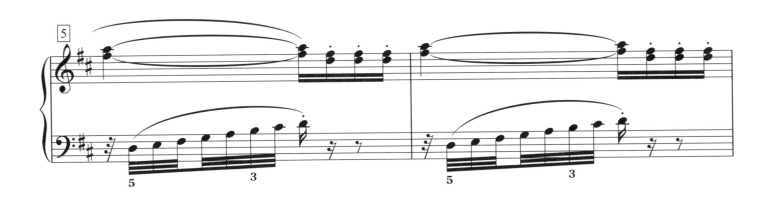

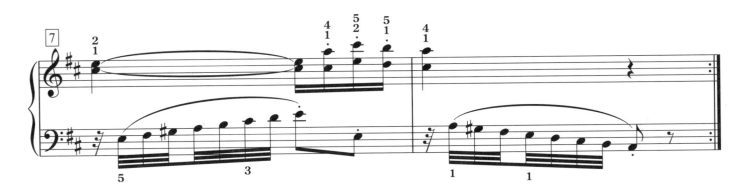

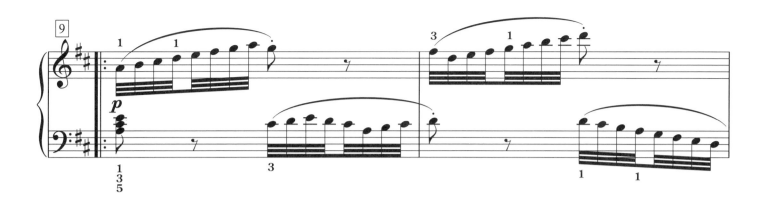

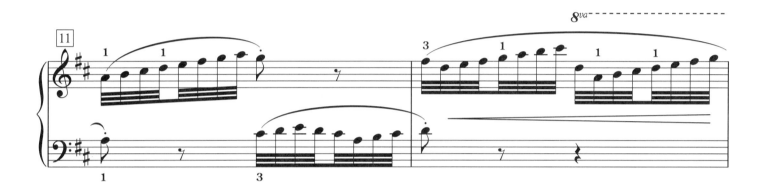

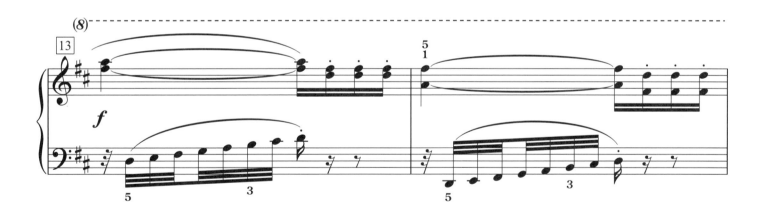

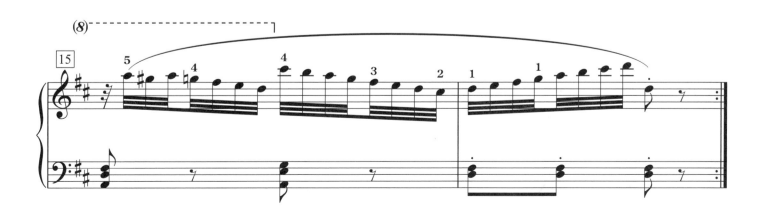

30

Op. 261, No. 58

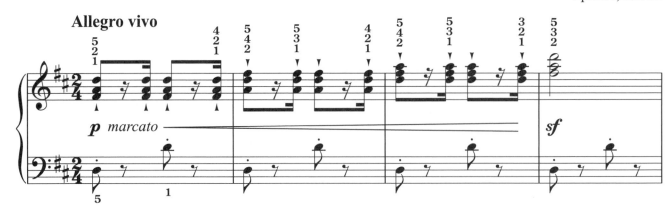

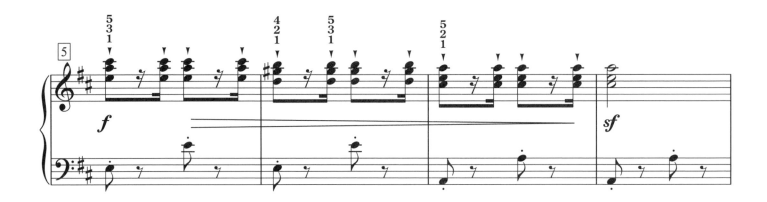

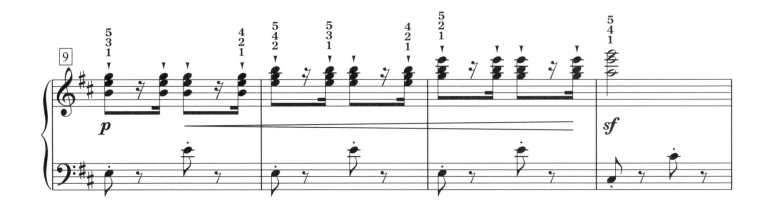

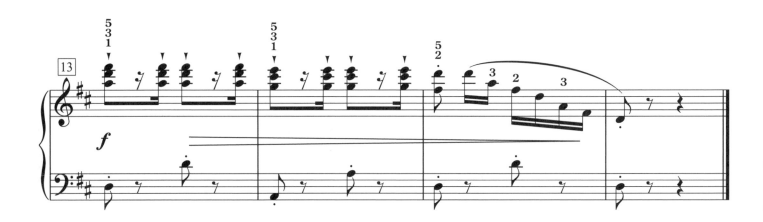

31

Op. 139, No. 70

Molto allegro

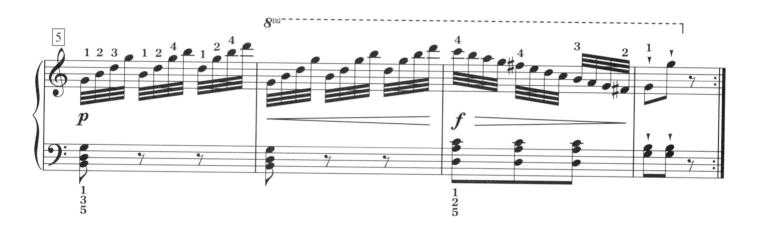

32

Op. 599, No. 61

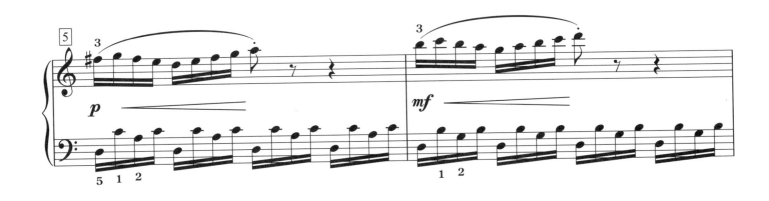

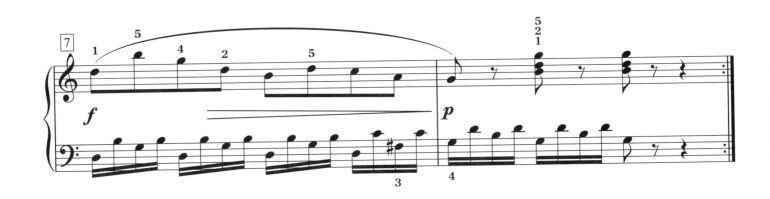

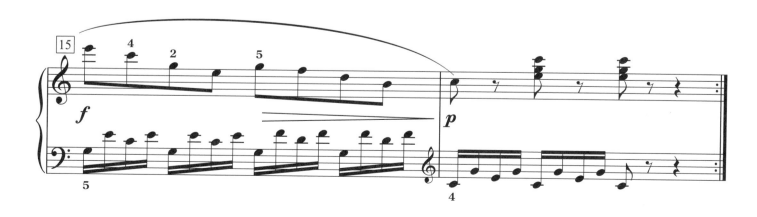

33

Op. 139, No. 59

Allegro ma non troppo

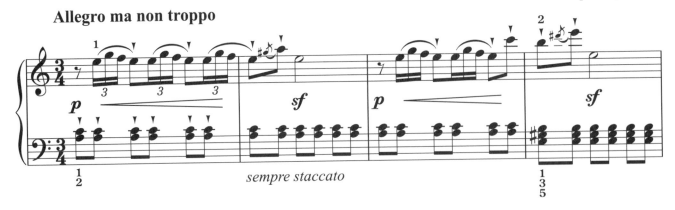

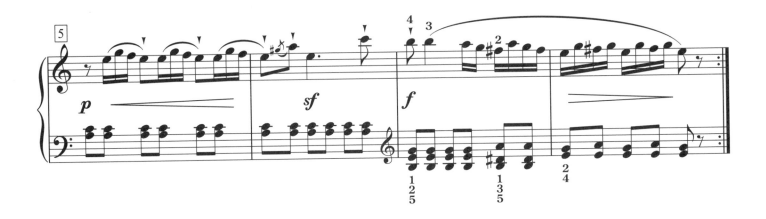

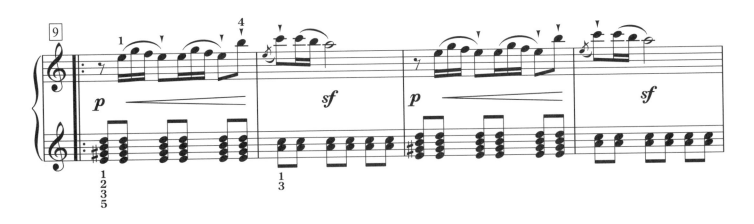

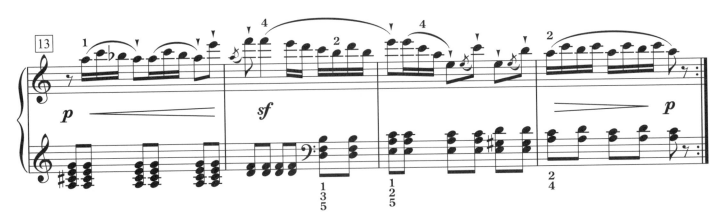

34

Op. 139, No. 58

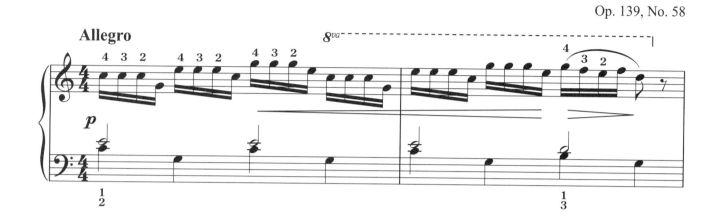

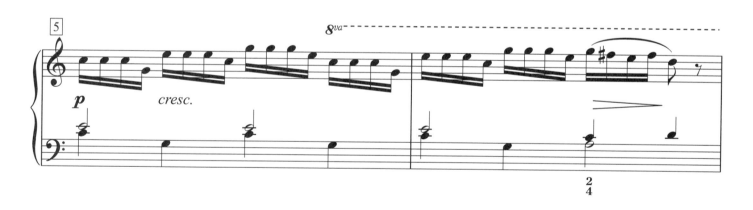

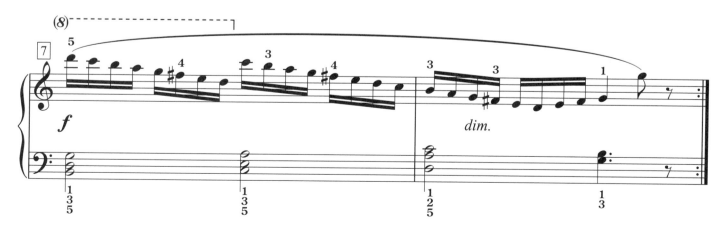

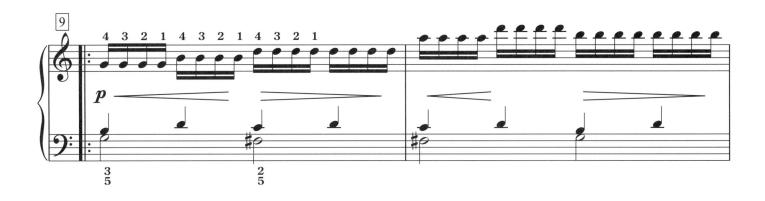

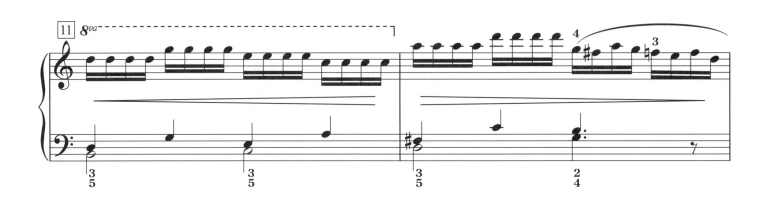

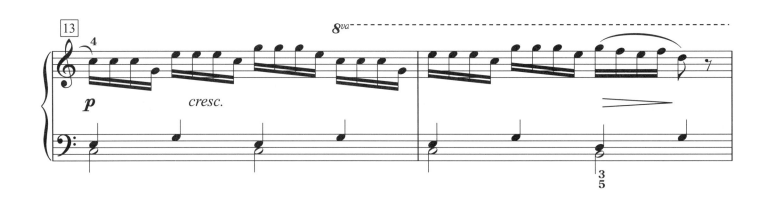

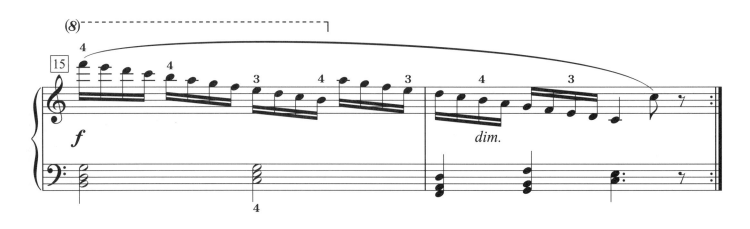

Op. 139, No. 71

Allegro vivo e scherzando

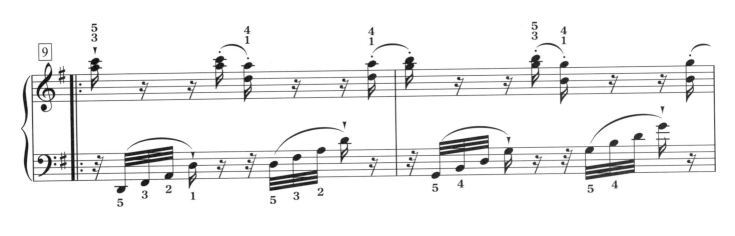

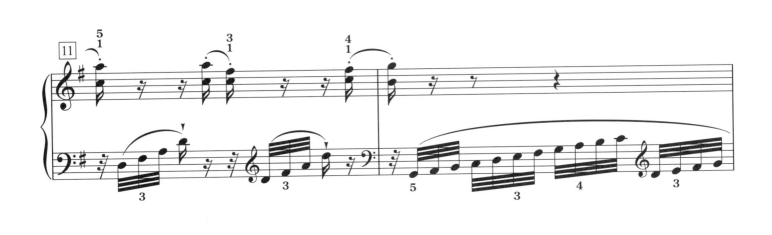

36

Op. 599, No. 57

37

Op. 599, No. 82

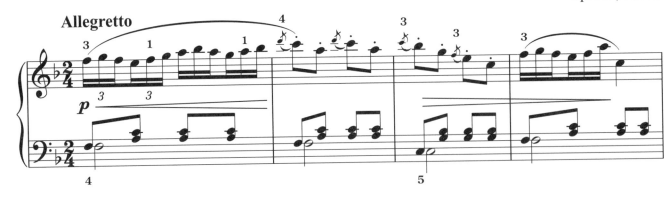

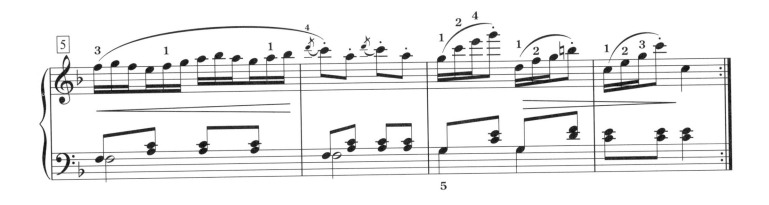

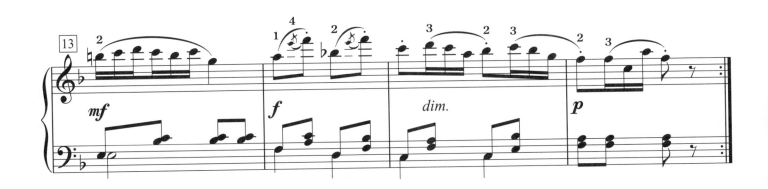

38

Allegro

Op. 599, No. 90

39

Op. 599, No. 60

Allegro

(con pedale)

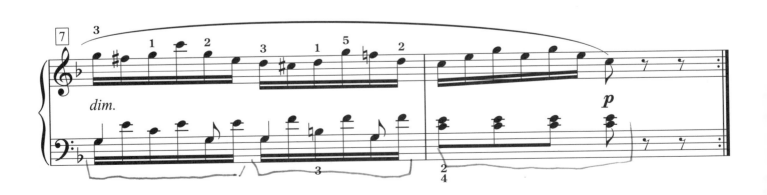

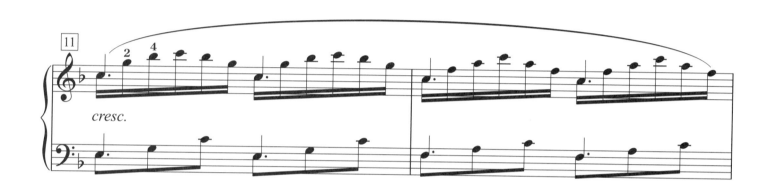

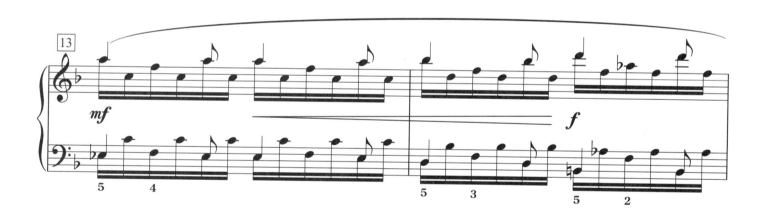

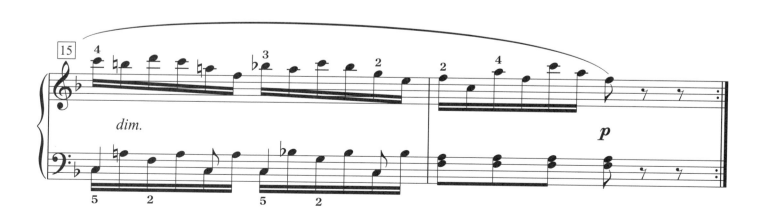

40

Op. 261, No. 54

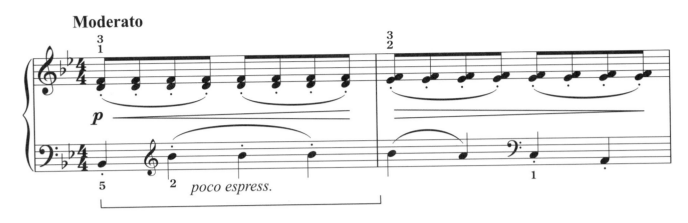

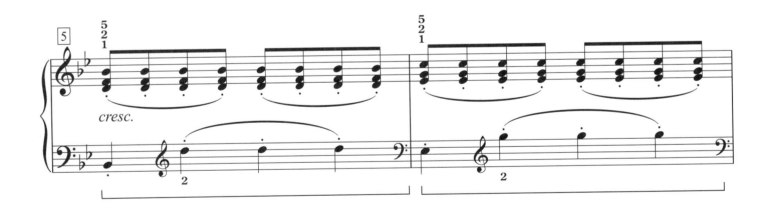

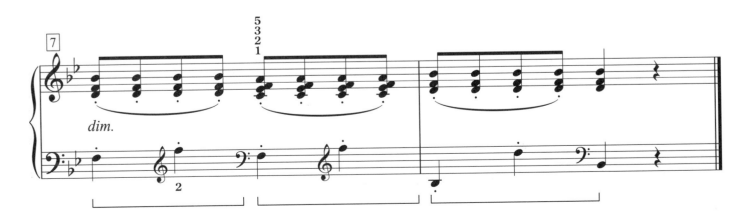

41

Op. 821, No. 12

Allegro moderato

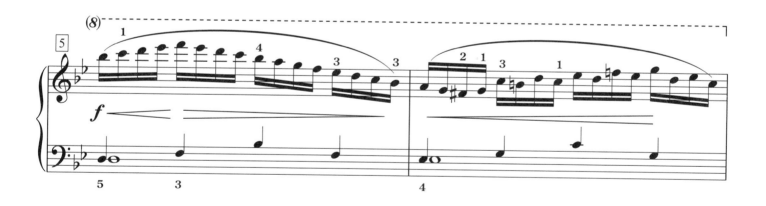

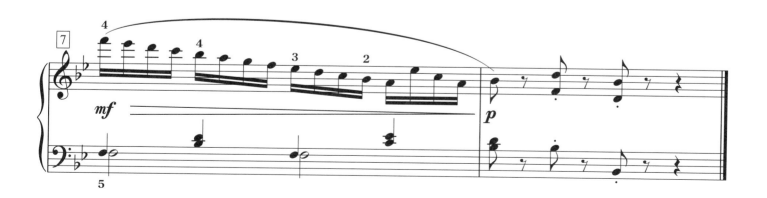

42

Op. 139, No. 75

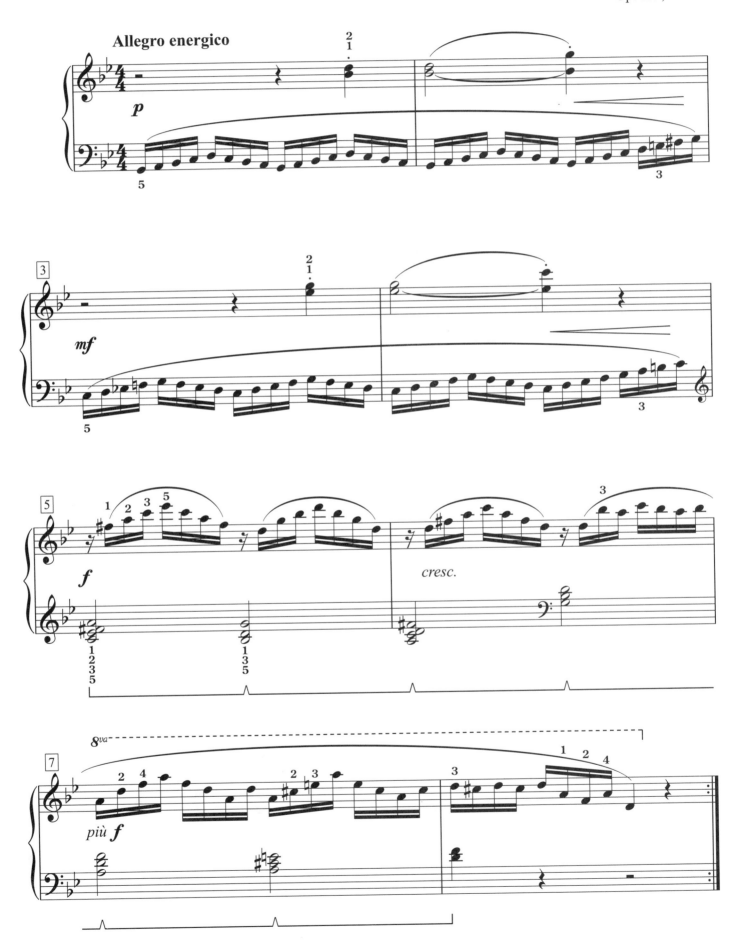

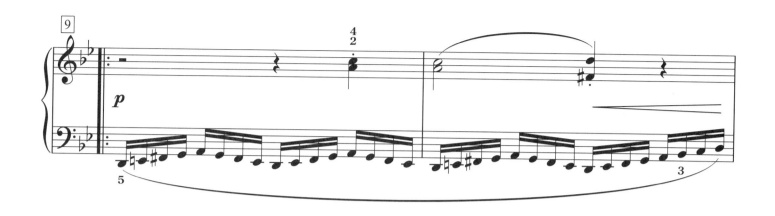

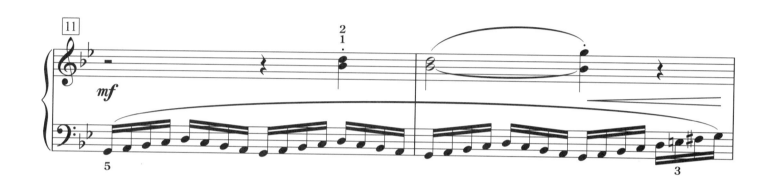

43

Op. 139, No. 36

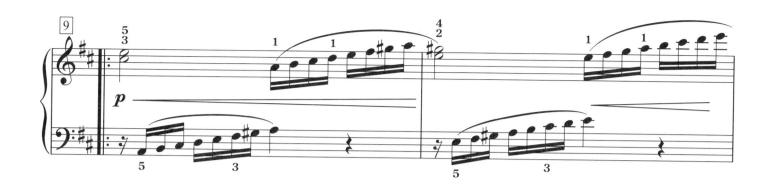

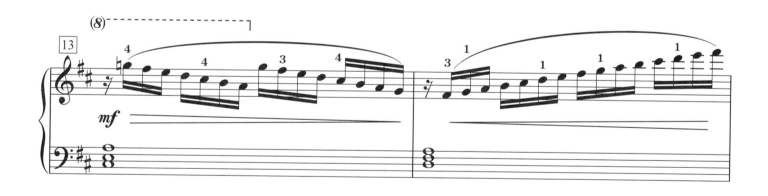

44

Op. 261, No. 53

45

Op. 599, No. 66

46

Op. 139, No. 95

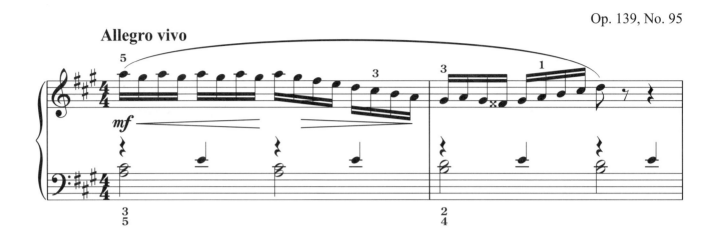

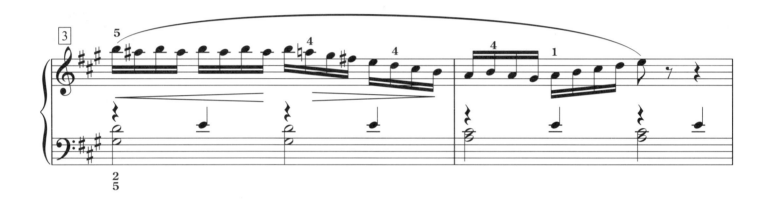

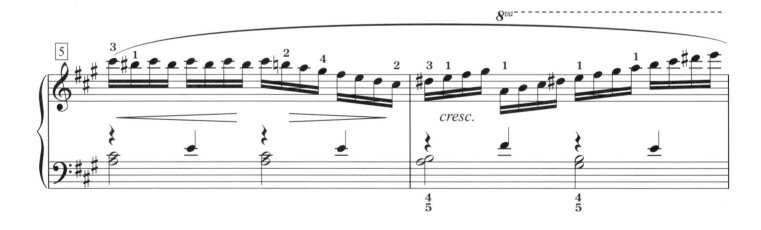

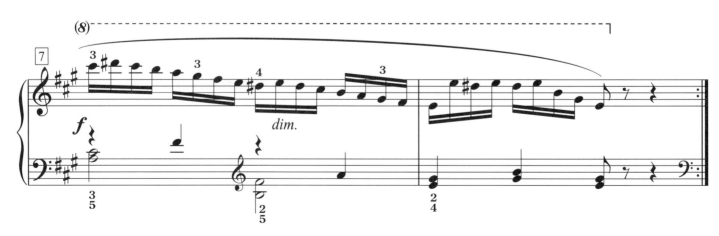

47

Op. 261, No. 47
Original Key: A-flat
Transposed by Germer

Allegro e leggiero

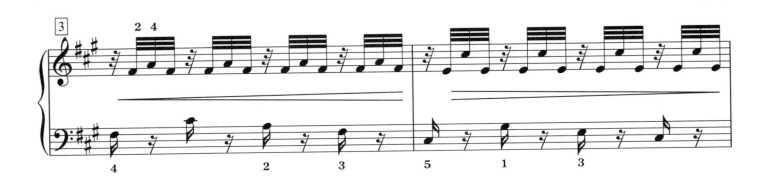

48

Op. 139, No. 97

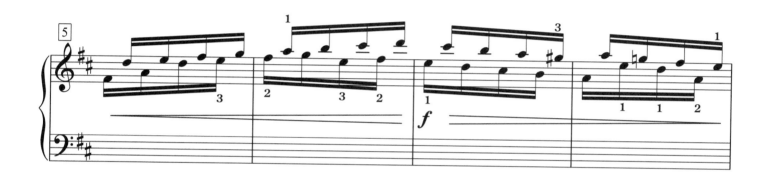

49

Op. 139, No. 98

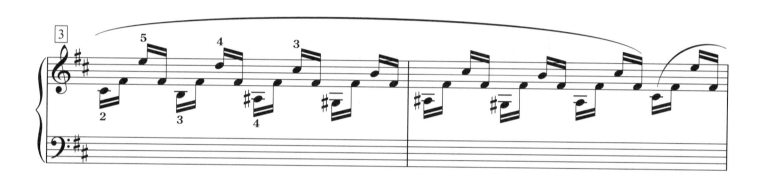

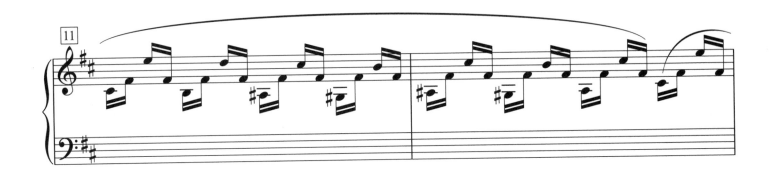

50

Op. 139, No. 100

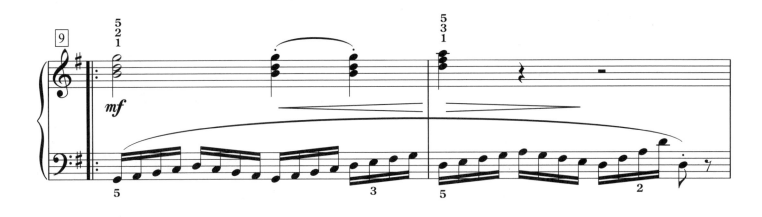

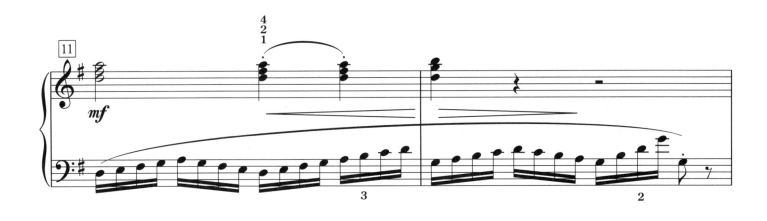

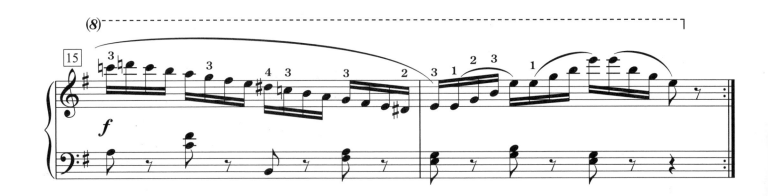